I0794238

ANIMAL BEHAVIOR

Rat Behavior

BY ANGELA LIM

Kids Core

An Imprint of Abdo Publishing
abdobooks.com

abdobooks.com

Published by Abdo Publishing, a division of ABDO, PO Box 398166, Minneapolis, Minnesota 55439. Copyright © 2024 by Abdo Consulting Group, Inc. International copyrights reserved in all countries. No part of this book may be reproduced in any form without written permission from the publisher. Kids Core™ is a trademark and logo of Abdo Publishing.

Printed in the United States of America, North Mankato, Minnesota.
052023
092023

THIS BOOK CONTAINS RECYCLED MATERIALS

Cover Photo: Irina Kozorog/Shutterstock Images
Interior Photos: Kirill Kurashov/Shutterstock Images, 4–5; Elena M. Tarasova/Shutterstock Images, 7; Chris Scuffins/Moment/Getty Images, 8; Shutterstock Images, 10, 17, 18, 24 (top left), 24 (top right), 24 (bottom right), 26, 28, 29 (bottom); Talya Photo/Shutterstock Images, 12–13; Carolyn A. McKeone/Science Source, 14; Ron Levine/DigitalVision/Getty Images, 20–21; Anna Hoychuk/Shutterstock Images, 22; Fabio Roberto De Andrade Filho/EyeEm/Getty Images, 23; Tanya Kim/Shutterstock Images, 24 (bottom left); Aneta Jungerova/Shutterstock Images, 29 (top)

Editor: Arnold Ringstad
Series Designer: Katharine Hale

Library of Congress Control Number: 2022949102

Publisher's Cataloging-in-Publication Data

Names: Lim, Angela, author.
Title: Rat behavior / by Angela Lim
Description: Minneapolis, Minnesota: Abdo Publishing Company, 2024 | Series: Animal behavior | Includes online resources and index.
Identifiers: ISBN 9781098291051 (lib. bdg.) | ISBN 9781098277239 (ebook)
Subjects: LCSH: Rats--Behavior--Juvenile literature. | Rats--Juvenile literature. | Rodents as pets--Juvenile literature. | Mammalogy--Juvenile literature.
Classification: DDC 591.51--dc23

CONTENTS

Rats are smart and social, and they are popular pets.

CHAPTER 1

Playtime with Hazel

Tommy looked into the cage of his new pet rat, Hazel. He and his dad had gotten Hazel last week. They watched as Hazel stood on her hind legs. Hazel squeaked at them and wiggled her nose.

Tommy's dad opened the cage. Hazel needed time to explore the room. Tommy and his dad watched to make sure Hazel stayed safe. Suddenly, a car outside honked. Hazel hid at the side of the room. Her ears were turned toward her tail. Tommy noticed Hazel looked tense.

Soon Hazel's **posture** began to relax. Tommy held out an apple piece to Hazel. The rat sniffed at the food. Hazel ate the apple and licked Tommy's hand. Tommy gently petted Hazel's head. Hazel's eyes bulged. Tommy's dad said this meant she was happy. Tommy was learning a lot about his new pet.

Apples are a common food for pet rats.

Learning about rat behavior can help people take better care of their rats.

What Is Behavior?

Behaviors are things people and animals do.

These actions are often used to **communicate**.

People may laugh when they are happy. They may scream when they are scared.

Rats and other animals use many behaviors to communicate. Rats can communicate by scent. For example, a rat can use its scent to mark its territory. It can produce a scent when it is ready to mate.

Rats also make sounds. Some rat noises are too high pitched for people to hear. People can hear lower-pitched rat noises, such as chirping.

Wide Awake

Rats are nocturnal. That means they are more active at night. They sleep during the day. Rat behaviors occur more often at night. Rats play more after the sun goes down.

Rats communicate with their owners in many ways.

Rats also have visual behaviors people can look for, including eye bulging.

Behaviors help rat owners understand their pets. People can look at their pets' actions. Then they can figure out how their pets are feeling. They learn what their pets need. They make sure their pets are happy and healthy.

Further Evidence

Look at the website below. Does it give any new evidence to support Chapter One?

10 Facts about Rats

abdocorelibrary.com/rat-behavior

Licking can be a sign of happiness in rats.

CHAPTER 2

Understanding Rat Behavior

Rats communicate in different ways than people do. But owners can watch and listen for certain behaviors. Doing so will help them take better care of their pets.

Grooming can mean a rat feels safe.

Feeling Friendly

Rats have many ways to show when they are feeling friendly. A relaxed rat may have droopy ears. It may lick its owner when it is happy.

Rats groom themselves. It is a sign of trust if a rat grooms itself in front of its owner. A rat may groom its owner to bond. But rats may also groom to **soothe** themselves when stressed. Owners should look at the body language of their rats for more clues.

Scent Marking

Rats use scent to mark their territory and belongings. They do this in two ways. First, they may rub against an object or person. Second, they may use urine as a scent marker. It can be a sign of attachment if a pet rat pees on its owner.

Other behaviors show friendliness too. A rat's teeth grow throughout its life. It grinds its teeth to keep them healthy. This behavior is called bruxing. An owner can hear when a rat grinds its teeth. Bruxing is a common sign of happiness. Eye bulging may happen with bruxing. This behavior is also called boggling. It means the rat is relaxed.

Sick or Unhappy

Rats change their behaviors when sick or stressed. A stressed rat has a tense posture. Its ears are alert. Its legs may be spread out. The rat is prepared to run.

A rat with a tense, alert posture may be ready to run.

The noises pet rats make can show how they are feeling.

Owners can listen to their pets. Rats may shriek when they are stressed or in pain. They may make quick, high-pitched sounds. Changes in noises can be a sign of illness. A loss of **appetite** is another sign.

Primary Source

Laurie Hess and Rick Axelson are veterinarians. They wrote about pet rats:

> [Rats] are extremely intelligent . . . interactive, and social. . . . If well socialized from a young age and treated gently, they are easy to handle, affectionate, and rarely bite.

Source: Laurie Hess and Rick Axelson. “Owning a Pet Rat.” *VCA Animal Hospitals*, 2022, vcahospitals.com. Accessed 26 July 2022.

What’s the Big Idea?

Read this quote carefully. What is its main idea? Explain how the main idea is supported by details.

Owners should pay close attention to make sure their rats feel safe.

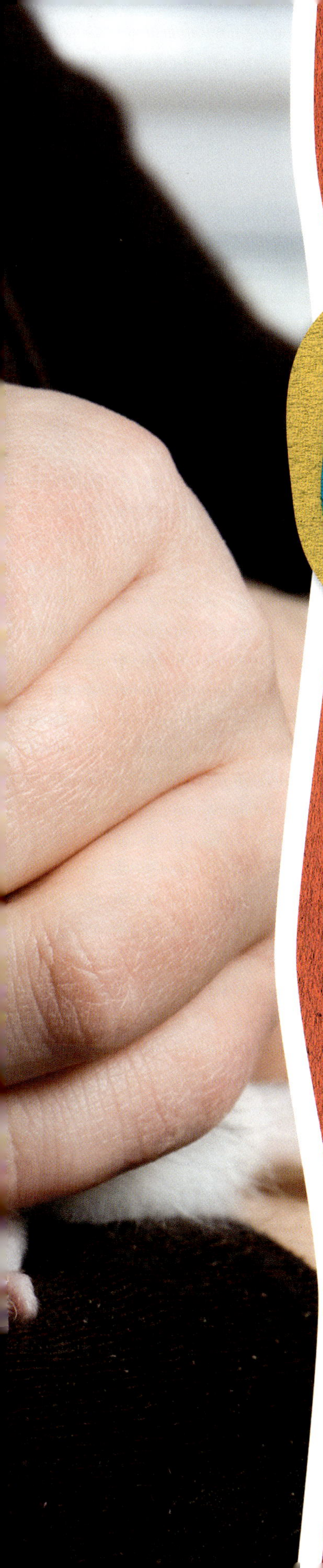

CHAPTER 3

Caring for Rats

Understanding rat behavior is an important part of caring for these pets. Some behaviors show that a rat is feeling friendly. Other behaviors mean a rat is stressed. An owner can check the pet's **environment**. The rat may fear something in its surroundings.

When rats are feeling happy, owners can feed them treats such as almonds by hand.

Time to Play

Rats may grind their teeth when they are happy. They have a relaxed posture. These behaviors can show that a rat is in a friendly mood.

Relaxed rats may play with or even climb on their owners.

Rat Care

Rat owners can make sure their pets are happy. Food and toys help increase friendly behaviors. Chances to explore outside the cage also help keep rats happy.

Owners can play with their pets when the rats are happy. They can feed their rats by hand.

An owner can pick up a rat when it is feeling relaxed. He or she can gently pet the rat.

This can strengthen the bond between an owner and a pet.

Building Trust

It takes time for people to build relationships with pets. They should be patient with a new rat. They should not force the pet to play if it is not ready. Toys and treats can help the rat adjust to its new home.

More Friends

Rats are social animals. They like to live in groups. Having two or more rats in a large cage can reduce a rat's stress. They can groom and play with each other.

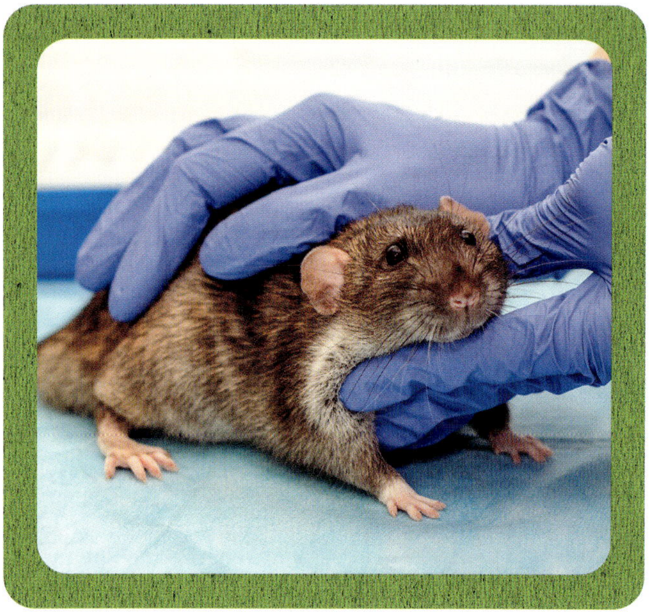

If a rat's behaviors suggest it might be sick, the owner can bring it to the vet.

A stressed rat may bite or scratch when handled. It does this because it is scared. Rat owners should make sure their rats have plenty of space. They can make sure the area is quiet so the pets feel safe. Long-term signs of stress, such as loss of appetite, may mean a rat is sick. Owners should then take their pets to the veterinarian. Knowing how rats communicate through behavior can help people take good care of their pets.

Primary Source

Megan LaFollette studies animal **welfare**. She has tickled rats for science. LaFollette spoke about these experiments:

> Rat tickling experiments show that . . . rats love [tickling.] It makes them happy, less afraid . . . and less stressed.

Source: Purdue Grad School. "Megan LaFollette - 3MT Competition 2019." *YouTube*, 2019, youtube.com. Accessed 26 July 2022.

Comparing Texts

Think about the quote. Does it support the information in this chapter? Or does it give a different perspective? Explain how in a few sentences.

Body Language

Stressed Behaviors

Friendly Behaviors

Glossary

appetite
an interest in eating

communicate
to share information through behavior or language

environment
the surroundings in which a person or animal lives

posture
a body position

soothe
to calm or bring comfort

welfare
the state of being healthy and happy

Online Resources

To learn more about rat behavior, visit our free resource websites below.

Core Library CONNECTION
FREE! COMMON CORE MULTIMEDIA RESOURCES

Visit **abdocorelibrary.com** or scan this QR code for free Common Core resources for teachers and students, including vetted activities, multimedia, and booklinks, for deeper subject comprehension.

Booklinks NONFICTION NETWORK
FREE! ONLINE NONFICTION RESOURCES

Visit **abdobooklinks.com** or scan this QR code for free additional online weblinks for further learning. These links are routinely monitored and updated to provide the most current information available.

Learn More

An, Priscilla. *Rabbit Behavior*. Abdo, 2024.

Davidson, Rose. *Squeak!* National Geographic Kids, 2019.

Pearson, Marie. *Dog Behavior*. Abdo, 2024.

Index

About the Author

Angela Lim is a writer and editor. She lives in Minnesota.